A Note to Parent

DK READERS is a compelling program for beginning readers, designed in conjunction with leading literacy experts, including Dr. Linda Gambrell, Professor of Education at Clemson University. Dr. Gambrell has served as President of the National Reading Conference, the College Reading Association, and the International Reading Association.

Beautiful illustrations and superb full-color photographs combine with engaging, easy-to-read stories and informational texts to offer a fresh approach to each subject in the series. Each DK READER is guaranteed to capture a child's interest while developing his or her reading skills, general knowledge, and love of reading.

The five levels of DK READERS are aimed at different reading abilities, enabling you to choose the books that are exactly right for your child:

Pre-level 1: Learning to read
Level 1: Beginning to read
Level 2: Beginning to read alone
Level 3: Reading alone
Level 4: Proficient readers

The "normal" age at which a child begins to read can be anywhere from three to eight years old. Adult participation through the lower levels is very helpful for providing encouragement, discussing storylines, and sounding out unfamiliar words.

No matter which level you select, you can be sure that you are helping your child learn to read, then read to learn!

LONDON, NEW YORK,
MELBOURNE, MUNICH, and DELHI

For DK/BradyGames
Global Strategy Guide Publisher
Mike Degler

Digital and Trade Category Publisher
Brian Saliba

Editor-In-Chief
H. Leigh Davis

Operations Manager
Stacey Beheler

Title Manager
Tim Fitzpatrick

Book Designer
Tim Amrhein

For DK Publishing
Publishing Director
Beth Sutinis

Licensing Editor
Nancy Ellwood

Reading Consultant
Linda B. Gambrell, Ph.D.

© 2011 Pokémon. © 1997–2011 Nintendo, Creatures, GAME
FREAK, TV Tokyo, ShoPro, JR Kikaku. Pokémon properties are
trademarks of Nintendo

DK/BradyGAMES
800 East 96th St., 3rd floor
Indianapolis, IN 46240

11 12 13 10 9 8 7 6 5 4 3 2 1

A catalog record for this book is available from the Library of Congress.

ISBN: 978-0-7566-5395-8 (Paperback)

ISBN: 978-0-7566-8666-6 (Hardback)

Printed and bound by Lake Book Manufacturing, Inc.

Discover more at

www.dk.com

DK READERS

BEGINNING
TO READ ALONE
2

Watch Out for Team Galactic!

Written by Michael Teitelbaum

DK Publishing

What is Team Galactic?

Who is Team Galactic?

Team Galactic is a group of villains. They want to destroy the universe and remake it into a place where they are in charge. Their leader is Cyrus. If Cyrus gets his way, he will become the supreme ruler of the universe. However, Cyrus is not in this alone.

The other main members of Team Galactic are Saturn, Mars, Jupiter, and Charon.

The Pokémon world is divided into many regions. Team Galactic does their dirty work in the Sinnoh region. At the center of this region is a huge mountain called Mt. Coronet.

When Pokémon Trainer Ash Ketchum first met Cyrus, Ash had no idea that Cyrus was the leader of Team Galactic. That's because Cyrus was also a rich businessman.

He was responsible for many buildings, including libraries, in the Sinnoh region.

Although Cyrus seems calm on the outside, he has a scheme to create what he feels would be an ideal world. This would be a world with no emotions and no chaos. It's up to Ash and his friends to stop Cyrus and the rest of Team Galactic from making Cyrus's dream come true.

Cyrus doesn't have any Pokémon of his own. However, he can always use Team Galactic's Golbat to do his evil bidding. In fact, Team Galactic uses swarms of Golbat to help them in their evil plans.

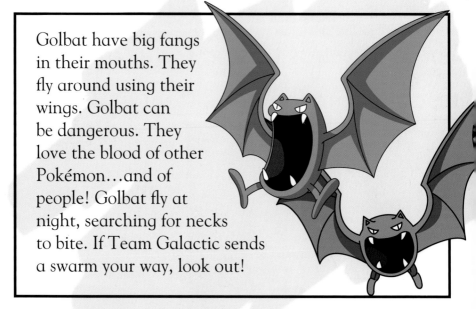

Golbat have big fangs in their mouths. They fly around using their wings. Golbat can be dangerous. They love the blood of other Pokémon…and of people! Golbat fly at night, searching for necks to bite. If Team Galactic sends a swarm your way, look out!

Cyrus needs the power of Sinnoh's Legendary Pokémon in order to complete his plan to create a new universe. That's why he wants to capture and control the Legendary Pokémon Uxie, Mesprit, Azelf, Dialga, and Palkia.

Cyrus also wants the Adamant Orb and the Lustrous Orb. These orbs have a mysterious power. Cyrus plans to combine these orbs with the power of the Lake Guardians, Uxie, Azelf, and Mesprit. Together, Cyrus needs them to summon the Legendary Pokémon, Dialga and Palkia. This must be done at a place called Spear Pillar.

Cyrus wants to control Dialga and Palkia too. Then he will use their power to create his new universe. To carry out Cyrus's plan, Team Galactic stops at nothing.

They even work with Team Rocket!

Jessie, James, and Meowth are members of Team Rocket. They want to steal other Trainers' Pokémon. You might think Team Rocket and Team Galactic get along. Actually, they don't! When Team Galactic wanted the Adamant Orb, they hired Team Rocket to steal it. Team Rocket failed. The next time the two teams met, Team Rocket opposed Team Galactic.

The two teams have been enemies
ever since.

Ash, Dawn, and Brock have battled
Team Rocket many times before.
Team Rocket are a familiar threat,
and not too bright. But Team Galactic
is more sinister and tougher to beat.

Saturn is one of Cyrus's main henchmen. He often leads missions and attacks for Team Galactic. He also hired Team Rocket to steal the Adamant Orb. Saturn is cool and calm. He thinks through every situation without getting emotional.

Eventually, Saturn realized that Cyrus

was using him for his own selfish purposes.

Saturn has two Pokémon: Bronzor and Toxicroak.

Like Saturn, they have fought many battles to help Team Galactic. Saturn used his Bronzor to help with Team Galactic's plan to steal the Lustrous Orb. Bronzor put the guards who were protecting the orb to sleep!

Saturn attempted to steal the many precious meteorites in Veilstone City. He knew that their power would help show Team Galactic where to go to summon Dialga and Palkia. This was how Ash and his friends encountered Team Galactic for the first time.

When Ash and his friends saw this, they sprang into action. Brock's Croagunk battled Saturn's Toxicroak. This began a long rivalry. Saturn's Toxicroak defeated Brock's Croagunk, but one day Croagunk would beat its rival.

By working together, the Trainers rescued most of the meteorites.

Team Galactic ran away, but their dirty work was far from finished.

Next, Team Galactic plotted to steal the Adamant and Lustrous Orbs from the Celestic Town Historical Research Center. This is a very important museum in Sinnoh. This is where Ash, Brock, and Dawn met Cyrus.

 He was still pretending to be a normal businessman.

Mars is another member of Team Galactic. She teamed up with Saturn to try to steal the orbs.

Mars is a troublemaker. She hopes that Cyrus's plan for a new universe actually succeeds. She also helped Team Galactic find Spear Pillar's location on Mt. Coronet.

Mars has two Pokémon: Purugly and Bronzor. Purugly helped Mars during her mission to Mt. Coronet. Purugly also created a distraction to fool Team Rocket.

Ash and his friends battled Mars and Saturn to keep them from getting the Lustrous Orb. It looked like Team Galactic would succeed in stealing the orb. Suddenly, Team Rocket escaped with it! Mars followed them. She and Jupiter battled Team Rocket and stole the Lustrous Orb back.

Jupiter is another of Cyrus's Team Galactic followers. Jupiter can be jealous, and she often complains. She was upset when the Lake Guardian Pokémon bonded with Ash and his friends instead of her and Team Galactic.

Jupiter has one main Pokémon: Skuntank. Skuntank, which can spray a bad-smelling liquid from its tail, took back the Lustrous Orb during Jupiter's battle with Team Rocket.

The next part of Team Galactic's plan depended on Charon. He is Team Galactic's technical expert. Charon cares only about himself. He thinks he is so much smarter and better than everyone else. His smug laugh often gets on his teammates' nerves.

Charon called himself "the brilliant genius." He had a plan to bring an item called the Red Chain back into the world. This would let Cyrus control Legendary Pokémon.

Without anyone's knowledge, Team Galactic recreated the Red Chain from the Veilstone meteorites.

Cyrus needed to gain control over the Legendary Pokémon. Team Galactic hired Pokémon Hunter J to catch Uxie, Mesprit, and Azelf. They are the three Legendary Pokémon known as the Lake Guardians.

Pokémon Hunter J is relentless and cruel. She steals Pokémon, and then sells them. She doesn't care if she hurts anyone in the process.

She is so greedy that nothing matters
to her except money.

She captured the Lake Guardians
and gave them to Team Galactic, but
these Pokémon were able to call for
help. They appeared to Ash, Dawn,
and Brock in a dream.

Ash, Dawn, and Brock wanted to help. So the Lake Guardians summoned Ash, Dawn, and Brock to them. The three friends appeared right in the middle of Team Galactic's base! Ash and his friends were trapped by Team Galactic. Then Cyrus used the Red Chain to take control of Uxie, Mesprit, and Azelf.

Cyrus ordered Ash, Dawn, and Brock to be thrown into a jail cell. Now the final part of his plan could begin.

At Spear Pillar, Cyrus combined the power of the orbs with the power of Uxie, Azelf, and Mesprit. He summoned the Legendary Pokémon, Dialga and Palkia. Cyrus then used the Red Chain to order Dialga and Palkia to create his new universe. The Pokémon obeyed, and a new universe opened up in front of him. However, the power that was unleashed threatened to destroy the world!

Cyrus had left Jupiter outside to guard Ash and his friends. Jupiter was upset that she had to stay behind. She wanted to see Cyrus's new universe.

Then before she knew it, Ash and his friends escaped.

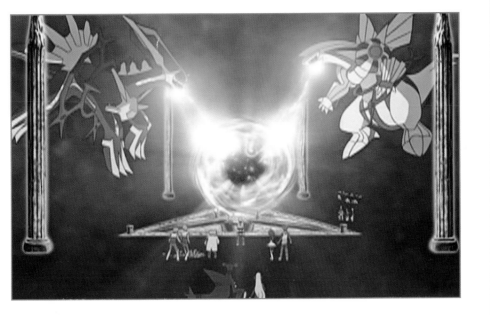

Ash, Dawn, and Brock arrived at
Spear Pillar just in time. Cyrus and
Team Galactic were about to achieve
their evil goal of creating a new
universe. Ash and his friends
battled Team Galactic. They freed
Uxie, Mesprit, and Azelf from
Cyrus's control.

The three Legendary Pokémon
connected their hearts with Ash,
Dawn, and Brock. Together, they
stopped Cyrus's new universe from
being completed. Then they freed
Dialga and Palkia. Ash, Dawn, and
Brock saved Sinnoh from destruction.

They helped arrest Team Galactic, but Cyrus got away. He vanished into his own universe.

Good Pokémon Trainers do more than catch and train Pokémon. They care for their Pokémon and create a friendship with them so that their Pokémon can thrive or even evolve.

Cyrus and Team Galactic dreamed of destroying the world. They hoped to create a new one with no place for caring, friendship, or love.

But thanks to Ash, Dawn, Brock, and their love of Pokémon, Team Galactic's evil plans were stopped.